AF571741

SUPERSTITIONS

BY
Suzanne Lord

Illustrated
by
Marion Krupp

New York

Library of Congress Cataloging-in-Publication Data
Lord, Suzanne.
Superstitions / by Suzanne Lord.
p. cm. — (Incredible histories.)
Includes bibliographical references.
Summary: Discusses the origins of many superstitions, including the fear of cats, the number thirteen, good luck charms, and walking under a ladder.
ISBN 0-89686-512-6
1. Superstition—Juvenile literature. 2. Superstition—History—Juvenile literature. [1. Superstition.] I. Title. II. Series.
BF1775.L67 1990
001.9'6—dc20 89-70867
CIP
AC

Illustration Credits
Cover: Kristi Schaeppi
Interior: Marion Krupp

Macmillan Publishing Company
866 Third Avenue
New York, NY 10022
Collier Macmillan Canada, Inc.

Printed in the United States of America

First Edition

10 9 8 7 6 5 4 3 2 1

Contents

What Are Superstitions?

Few people admit they are superstitious. And few people will walk under a ladder rather than around one. Superstitions are as old as humankind itself. From the Stone Age to the nuclear age, people have held two equally strong and opposite beliefs. One belief is that people are at the mercy of forces they cannot control. The second belief is that people can control these forces if only they know how. So according to one theory, superstitions are trial-and-error attempts to figure out how to control the uncontrollable.

A superstition results from a belief in or fear of what is unknown, mysterious, or supernatural. Superstitions are usually attempts to *control* what is unknown, mysterious, or supernatural.

Superstitions give some people the feeling that they can control their fate. Certain actions, some people hope, will ward off evil and bring good. Whether superstitious acts seem to work or not, many people keep repeating them — just in case.

Ancient Humans and Their World

Ancient humans lived on what they found, killed, or could grow. Good or bad luck could mean the life or death of an entire tribe. Hunting was a vital part of ancient life. Tribe members would notice what they did, wore, or said on days of bad hunting and on days of good hunting. Next time, people would repeat what they had done on good hunting days. They would avoid doing things they had done on bad hunting days. Eventually, this led to strict rites and ceremonies performed before every hunt.

In the ancients' view of the world, invisible but powerful spirits controlled nature. What a person did could please a spirit or make it angry. An angry spirit brought evil that could make people sick or crazy. An angry spirit might also make crops die. A spirit might make herd animals sick or bring on droughts or floods. A pleased spirit, on the other hand, could reveal great secrets such as fire or a way to make stronger weapons. Sometimes a pleased spirit would bring a much-needed rainfall.

Ancient peoples believed that certain things, as well as certain actions, could repel evil spirits and attract good ones. Various objects were set around a home to keep evil away. Others were worn around the neck to attract good spirits.

Dead people were thought to be dangerous, in ancient times. When the body died, a person became a spirit. The spirit was jealous of the living and was able to do them harm. Many burial customs came about from early attempts to put the dead in their places and keep them there. Corpses were tied or shut in boxes. They were "held down" with spirit-repelling forces (iron, for instance, including iron coffin nails). The dead people's favorite objects were buried with them so they would not come back looking for anything. Then they were buried under heavy loads of dirt and kept in place with heavy stone slabs.

Modern People — Or Are We?

Though our methods have changed, modern people are still trying to tip the balance of the universe in our favor. Good spirits have come to be called good luck. Rites, ceremonies, and amulets have turned into superstitions, customs, and lucky charms. But we still have a lot in common with our Stone Age ancestors.

A baseball player who has a great game after eating a certain brand of sausage makes sure he has that brand before every game. His superstition is similar to an ancient hunting ritual.

Many people still seem to believe in powerful, invisible forces. When the horoscope section of a newspaper was accidentally left out one day, the paper's newsroom received over 500 angry calls and letters. Apparently, many people did not feel they could get through their day without knowing what the stars had in store for them.

Black Cats Crossing Our Paths

Cats of the Past

One common superstition is that bad luck will come to anyone whose path is crossed by a black cat. How did this belief come about?

One of ancient Egypt's most powerful goddesses was a cat. Her name was Bast. Her festivals were attended by people from all over the country.

Bast loved music, dancing, good wine, and jokes. In her honor, Egyptians indulged their cats. They decorated them with jewelry. When the cats died, Egyptians mummified them like humans. In 500 B.C., an attacking Persian army arrived in Egypt. Every Persian soldier was carrying a cat. The Egyptian city of Memphis surrendered. The Egyptians did not want to shoot at the Persians and possibly kill any cats.

Greeks and Romans did not worship the cat. But they did feel there was something godlike about the aloof, graceful animal.

Norse mythology, however, made much of the cat. Again, the cat was identified with a woman. This time the goddess was Freya. Her chariot was drawn by two cats. Freya had many love affairs that were like a cat's — at night and often. Thus, cats became identified with love and Friday (Freya's day) through Norse mythology.

Fear of the Dark

Fear of the dark is one of our deepest and oldest fears. We are creatures of daytime. We do not like to be where we cannot see what is going on. We think unknown things lurk in the dark. Even the light of the moon was once thought to be harmful. The Latin word for moon is *luna.* At one time, a full moon was thought to cause lunacy.

Cats are active at night. They hunt and make weird noises. Their eyes shine in the dark. Cats love to rub up against objects. When they do this at night, static electricity sometimes causes their fur to throw off starlike sparks in the dark. For these reasons, cats became identified with nighttime. And black cats, in particular, seem most like the night.

Beginning in medieval times, cats began to be associated with magic and evil. Cats were part of the old religions that Christianity was trying to get rid of. These creatures became identified with witches. Christians believed witches could change into black cats because black was the color of the devil. This association still holds. In many Halloween decorations, witches are shown with their trusty black cats. For witches to be without their cats is as unthinkable as for them to appear without their flying broomsticks!

Over the course of several centuries, cats had gone from being gods to being servants of the devil.

Cats in Our Lives

Today, people do not think cats are agents of the devil. But cats still have a faint tinge of bad luck about them. For years, Europeans would not let a child sleep with a cat in the crib. Superstition said that at night the cat would suck the breath out of the baby.

Cats have a dual nature that disturbs some people. The fact is, that lovely purring creature is also a cold-blooded killer. A recent study showed the effect of house cats in an English village on the local bird and rodent population. The "head count" of cat-caused deaths was astonishing.

Even today, when some people see a cat, they think of darkness and witches. Without really believing that a black cat crossing their path is bad luck, they move aside. Why take chances?

Do You Have Triskaidekaphobia?

Triskaidekaphobia (tris-ki-dek-a-fō-be-a) means a fear of the number 13. But why would people fear a number?

Humans are the only creatures on earth that are able to count. Because humans have always been superstitious, they soon attached meaning to numbers. Some numbers were good, some were bad.

Different Numbers in History

The number three has always been popular. Greeks and Egyptians liked three and its multiples. Egyptians gave the cat nine lives (three times three). Greeks gave us twelve months of the year and two twelve-hour units of time for the day (three times four). They also left us measurements of twelve: Twelve inches equal one foot, goods come in "grosses" (twelve times twelve), even eggs come in dozens. Religious Europeans liked three as well. The Christian Trinity has three parts. Fairy tales grant three wishes and tell of three little pigs or three blind mice. We eat three meals a day to keep healthy. Traditionally, we take medicines three times a day, before or after meals. The ancient Chinese believed that heaven came in three parts, each three times as big as the part below it. Temples had three entrances.

The number four has also been popular. Native Americans hold their ceremonies and sing ceremonial songs in sets of four. In the Middle Ages, scholars developed concepts about the four elements (earth, air, fire, and water), the four seasons, and the four winds.

The Bible is fond of the number forty. Noah's flood went on for forty days and forty nights. Jesus, Moses, and Elijah all fasted for forty days. Moses's tribe wandered forty years in the desert. Jesus spent forty days on earth between his resurrection and final ascension. Saul, David, and Solomon each reigned forty years.

Some people believe that the number six is special because it is the sum of one, two, and three. The number eight is bad news—Greeks believed it was the number of death. The phrase "behind the eight ball" means someone is in a tough spot. Another bad number is two. English legend says a king with a Roman numeral two after his name will come to a bad end. The deuce is a bad card, and snake eyes is a loser in dice.

But two numbers in superstitious lore stand out—the numbers 13 and 7.

The Number 13 and Friday the 13th

The number 13 is considered unlucky because it is the number of people who sat at the Last Supper on the night Judas betrayed Jesus.

People leery of 13 will not stay on the 13th floor or rent a room with 13 on the door. Some tall buildings—including hotels—do not even have a 13th floor. Their floor numbers go from 12 to 14.

According to *Smithsonian* magazine, fear of the number 13 "costs America a billion dollars a year in absenteeism, train and plane cancellations, and reduced commerce on the 13th of the month." The French would rather hire a *quatorzième* (a professional 14th guest) than hold a dinner party with 13 people at the table. Napoleon, J. Paul Getty, Herbert Hoover, and Franklin Delano Roosevelt all avoided eating at tables where 13 people were present.

In April 1970, an Apollo spaceflight was aborted. Was it because something went wrong with the equipment? No, insisted triskaidekaphobics. The mission was "cursed" with a run of 13s! It was the 13th mission, launched from pad 39 (13 times 3) at 1:13 P.M. (1313 in military time) on April 13.

Friday has a bad reputation because it was the day Jesus was crucified. Therefore, Fridays are for endings, not beginnings. It used to be the traditional day for hangings. Superstition dictates that Friday is a bad day to get married, begin a trip, move into a new house, or start a new job. What could be worse than Friday the 13th? Not much, say triskaidekaphobics.

America has mixed feelings about the number 13. After all, we had 13 original colonies. *E pluribus unum* has 13 letters. And the United States seal is studded with 13s. It has 13 stars and 13 bars. There are 13 feathers in the eagle's tail, 13 bars in one claw, and 13 olives in the branches held in the other claw.

Thirteen New York men got together and started the Thirteen Club on a Friday the 13th in 1882. They met in room number 13 of the Knickerbocker Club. Meetings began at 8:13. They dined 13 at a table on the 13th of each month and told "lucky" stories about the number 13. The initiation fee was $1.13. Monthly dues were 13¢. A lifetime membership was $13. Branch clubs paid $13.13 for a charter membership. The club had thirteen hundred members at one point, including such people as President Chester A. Arthur and P. T. Barnum.

The Number Seven

From ancient Babylonian times on, seven has been the number of virtue and perfection. Babylonians, who lived around the year 2500 B.C., had seven winds and seven zones of the under- and upper worlds. They were the first to reserve every seventh day for religious observance and rest.

Ancient Greeks added two favorite numbers (three and four) to find perfection in seven. They had seven sages and seven wonders of the world. They believed each person's basic temperament was "set" during his or her seventh year.

Some Hindus washed the bride and bridegroom on their marriage morning. They used water from seven different village wells. The water was brought by seven happily married women. Arabs took oaths on seven blood-smeared stones. They believed in seven heavens, the seventh being the best. From that, we say that a really happy person is in seventh heaven!

Medieval Europeans took the heavenly number three and the earthly number four to express the entire universe in the number seven. This universe had seven planets and seven circles of heaven. Humans were divided into seven bodily parts. A belief that persists today is that the seventh son of a seventh son has special healing powers.

Good Luck Charms

One way of bringing "Lady Luck" to a person's door is to attract her with good luck charms. The belief that an object can be lucky is an old one. Certain stones, coins, and plant or animal parts may be carried, touched, or worn. These charms luck may bring good fortune or repel something bad.

Lucky Rabbit's Foot

The rabbit as a good luck omen goes back to ancient times. People noticed that rabbits produced more rabbits with rapid frequency. Owning a rabbit, seeing a rabbit, or carrying around part of a rabbit, they said, might cause your money, business, or family to increase.

A woman who wants a big family is supposed to carry a rabbit's foot. A rabbit's foot laid on a newborn child is good luck. A rabbit's foot in one's pocket helps ease some pain. French superstition says that a hare's foot placed under the left armpit keeps a person from having toothaches.

Generally, though, a rabbit's foot is carried for good luck. If your rabbit's foot isn't working, it may be because you have a fake one. Some people say a rabbit's left foot will bring good luck. Some say you need a left hind foot. Others say the best rabbit's foot is one from an animal killed by a cross-eyed person during a full-moon night!

The Lucky Horseshoe

In ancient times, the crescent shape was considered magical. It's little wonder that the crescent-shaped horseshoe got a little magic shed on it. Though leather bootics had been used on racehorses, the Romans later began using iron horseshoes. Iron is supposedly a metal the devil and his witches do not like. Thus, iron horseshoes have the reputation of being able to repel evil.

Some people say Saint Dunstan, a tenth-century English monk, is responsible for the devil's dislike of horseshoes. In many traditions the devil has goatlike cloven hooves instead of feet. Legend says the devil asked Dunstan to shoe his hooves. Saint Dunstan did, but he made sure the shoeing hurt the devil's hooves. The devil promised if Saint Dunstan would stop the pain, he and his servants would never go near horseshoes again.

Horseshoes are traditionally put over house doors as witch repellants. They are also nailed over barn doors, roof beams, stable doors, and on children's cradles.

The Pennsylvania Dutch hang their horseshoes heel down so luck will be spilled into the house. Other people hang horseshoes heel up so luck will never spill out.

Miniature horseshoes may be carried by brides or grooms. Sometimes wedding cakes or congratulatory cards are decorated with horseshoe shapes. Sometimes confetti cut into the shape of horseshoes is thrown at newlyweds, instead of rice.

Four-Leaf Clover

Finding a four-leaf clover in a field is a rare occurrence. This in itself makes it seem lucky. Medieval Christians felt this cross-shaped clover was extra lucky. One superstition says that when Adam and Eve were thrown out of the Garden of Eden, the only thing Eve took was a four-leaf clover. As the only plant left from the perfect garden, it is luckier than ever!

"Being in clover" means you are having a great run of luck or have made a financial gain. Girls used to put four-leaf clovers in each corner of their bed sheets to help them dream about their future husbands.

Four-leaf clovers have been lucky for one group of people — the horticulturists who grow and sell them! "Due to the superstitious demand of millions of Americans," one magazine article stated, "growing four-leaf clovers has developed into a large industry."

All's Fair in Love

Courtship Superstitions

Most future-spouse superstitions and marriage rites center on women. In olden times, the choice of a marriage partner might be the only major decision permitted a woman during her life. The decision would make or break her future. Choosing the wrong suitor and ending up in a bad marriage meant an entire life of suffering. Young women were interested in superstitions that promised a peek at their future spouses!

One common fortune-telling ritual was to take the seeds out of an apple and give each a suitor's name. The girl would then put the seeds on her cheeks while they were still wet. The seed that stuck the longest named her future husband. Another superstition involved letting a snail crawl through ashes overnight. The snail would leave a trail wherever it crawled that night. In the morning, a girl would look at the trail. Whatever letter the snail's trail seemed to form would be the initial of her future spouse.

Some girls slept with a silver spoon, a mirror, a little ladder of sticks, a piece of someone else's wedding cake, or three pebbles from a place they had never been before. The girls thought they would dream about their future husbands. Some peeled apples so that they made long, unbroken peels. They twirled them around their heads three times and tossed them on the floor. When the peels hit the floor, they would form the initials of their future husbands.

A person who stumbled while walking upstairs would marry soon. The closer the stumbler was to the top of the stairs, the sooner the wedding would be. A person who felt like sneezing but could not knew that someone loved him or her but was too shy to say so.

A sure way to see one's future husband was to hold a "silent supper." This ritual involved several girls. Everything was done backward. The food was served backward and place settings and chairs were set backward.

No one spoke a single word. Just before midnight, the girls would back up and sit in their backward chairs. They stared into the darkness. At midnight, they would see their future husbands walking toward them or standing in front of them.

Superstitions in Wedding Customs

Good luck at the beginning of an important event is supposed to bring good luck to the rest of that event. Since one of the most important events of a person's life is a wedding, there are many superstitions attached to weddings. These superstitions are supposed to start the new couple out on the right track to a happy and lucky life together.

Superstitious people might feel it is bad luck to hold a wedding at a serious time, such as Lent. They may not want to hold it on an unlucky day, such as Friday. The couple may feel it is lucky to walk uphill to the marriage place. This way their life will head in an upward, not a downward, course. The bride might be careful not to wear anything black that day, because black is an unlucky color. The groom might be careful not to accept any telegram that day. Sometimes telegrams bring bad news, and this would be bad luck on a wedding day.

Of course, not every couple will obey every superstition. But most new couples follow one or more superstitions "just for luck."

Wedding customs are full of superstitions. Many of these superstitions are so old that we have forgotten their meanings. Here are some wedding customs that most new couples follow today and the history behind them.

JUNE WEDDING: Ancient Rome is the origin of many wedding customs. The ancient Romans married in the month of June because that month was dedicated to Juno, their queen of heaven. Marrying in June became a custom that has continued to the present day, 2,000 years later.

CUTTING THE WEDDING CAKE: In many ancient cultures, sharing food was a symbol that the newlyweds would share their lives and their goods. Today the tradition of cutting the wedding cake has the same symbolic meaning. The newly married couple holds a cake-cutting knife together to show that they will work together in their marriage. Then they cut the first piece of the wedding cake and eat it together.

THE BEST MAN AND MAID OF HONOR: In medieval Europe people believed the devil hated happiness and wanted to hurt the happy new couple. But if two similarly dressed happy couples stood close to one another at the ceremony, the devil would become confused and leave. Even though this superstition is no longer believed, weddings still include a best man and maid of honor to "stand in" for the new couple.

THROWING RICE: This custom also began in medieval Europe as a way to ward off evil spirits. As the happy couple left the church, their guard was down. They were in danger of being taken advantage of by evil spirits. But the spirits were gluttons who could not pass up a snack. The couple "escaped" in the hail of food thrown to distract the spirits. Today, nobody believes they are fooling evil spirits by throwing rice. In fact, at today's weddings confetti is sometimes thrown. But the custom remains a staple of traditional weddings.

CARRYING THE BRIDE OVER THE THRESHOLD: In former times, the household was the woman's domain. How she entered her new home set up her entire future in it. Tripping over the threshold was a very bad omen. To avoid it, the groom carried his new bride over the threshold. Today this custom survives as a romantic tradition.

Oops! Bad Luck!

The Evil Eye

Bad luck is something people want to avoid. Some say bad luck comes from one of two places: the devil and his helpers, or the evil eye.

Avoiding the evil eye is the basis for many superstitions. An envious person stares at a lucky one and wishes him or her ill. This malicious stare, or "evil eye," is supposed to bring bad luck to its victims. (In fact, the word *envy* comes from the Latin expression *in videre*, meaning "to look in the eye.") This evil stare captures its victim and can bring on anything from a run of bad luck to the victim's death.

Spilled Salt

In ancient times, salt was the main preservative. Thus, salt represented things that one wanted to preserve. Friendship, one's home, or one's sworn word were all things people wanted to preserve.

Romans placed a high value on salt. It was sometimes used as payment. We get our word *salary* from *sal*, the Roman word for salt. Romans always put salt on their tables first and removed it last. They thought it protected their homes. Spilling it was considered bad luck.

But why, when salt is spilled, does one throw a pinch over the left shoulder? After all, some say the left side is one's "bad" side. (The Latin word for left is *sinister.*)

The left side of the body has had a bad reputation since the ancient Greek era. Most people, then and now, are right handed. In battle, swords were held in the right hand. Two right-handed swordsmen were in a normal fighting position. But left-handed swordsmen threw fights off balance. Left-handed swordsmen had lots of practice fighting "righties." But right-handers had not fought many left-handed people. Thus, a left-handed fighter was a dangerous person to run into. Danger is bad luck.

Soon the left side itself became associated with bad luck. Some people felt it was bad luck to start a journey on the left foot, or to start the day by putting the left shoe on first.

In olden times people felt that evil spirits lurked behind a person's left side. Spilling salt made a person vulnerable to these spirits. Throwing a pinch of salt over

the left shoulder scared away the evil spirits. It canceled out the bad luck of the spill. When people spill salt today, they don't worry about evil spirits. But they still throw a pinch over their left shoulders "just for luck."

Walking Under a Ladder

Here is a superstition that everyone knows. Ladders are symbols of going somewhere — either up or down. Dreaming of climbing up a ladder means you will reach great heights in life. Dreaming of climbing down means you will lose money.

Tradition says a ladder was leaning against Jesus' cross. The devil stood underneath that ladder. He was angry because he had lost all the souls Jesus' sacrifice saved. "Under the ladder" became Satan's territory. Walking under one puts a person in danger of the devil's ambush.

In ancient Asian countries, criminals were hanged from the seventh rung of ladders if no tree limbs were available. Passing under a ladder from which a person had been hanged could put one in contact with that person's ghost.

Breaking a Mirror

To ancient folk, mirrors were dangerous. They "caught" an image of the original person and "made" two of the person. If one of the doubles was to enter the realm of the other, all sorts of havoc could happen. That is why mirrors are covered over in a room when someone has died. Some people believe the soul of the deceased might wander into the mirror and get lost on its way to heaven. Many people cover mirrors while they sleep. They do not want their spirits to wander into the mirrors and get trapped outside their bodies!

Romans, who loved the number seven, believed the body "renewed" itself every seven years. A broken mirror hurt the image of the person looking into it. It canceled that person's renewal. That is where the idea of seven years' bad luck came from.

Good Luck

Most people would want good fortune all the time if they could get it. But most of us cannot get it. The following are a few superstitions people have used and still use to tip the odds in favor of good luck.

Knock on Wood

In times past, trees were thought to contain spirits or gods. Druids (Celtic priests) in particular believed that oak was holy. They worshiped in sacred oak groves.

Wood became linked with sacred protection. People began to touch or knock wood when they hoped for a positive outcome. Most people touch or knock anything made of wood — a table, chair, or door. As a joke, some people knock their "wooden" heads. But some U.S. Air Force crews, whose lives depend on their machinery staying in the air, insist on touching or knocking trees before taking off on missions.

Lucky Foods on New Year's Day

We have already seen how important beginnings are in superstitious lore. People feel an enterprise that begins lucky will stay lucky. New Year's is the first day of the year. Superstitious people feel what one does on New Year's Day affects whether the rest of the year will be good or bad.

Having enough of everything to get through the next year has always been a prime concern for people. Superstitions have been used to help bring this about.

On New Year's Eve, some people put a loaf of bread, some salt, and a silver dollar on their kitchen tables. This means that for the coming year their families will have enough food, good luck, and money.

Some people bring cakes or loaves of bread home on New Year's Day to ensure prosperity. They do not have empty pockets or empty cupboards. Superstition says they must not let fires die out on New Year's Day.

The Japanese bake eight cakes on New Year's for the sun and moon goddesses. For good luck, northern Europeans used to eat cakes shaped like boars.

Black-eyed peas and hog jowl are the traditional "good luck" menu in the southern United States. In other areas, people eat cabbage. Still others eat green beans and dried peas on New Year's Day. They think they will have "greenback and silver all the way." Most food superstitions depend on having some kind of food that swells up when cooked. If you eat food that has swelled up, your pocketbook will swell up all year.

Gesundheit!

In ancient times, people did not know about germs. They thought diseases came from evil spirits or the evil eye. The best way to stay well was to wear something to repel evil influences. Garlic was a frequent choice. Egyptians fed large doses of garlic to their laborers to keep them well. For centuries, garlic cloves were hung around the necks of children to keep away spirits causing illness. It probably worked in the case of contagious diseases. The garlic smelled so bad it kept everyone away. The use of garlic as vampire repellant comes from its supposed anti-evil qualities.

Sneezing has been considered a dangerous activity for centuries. During a sneeze, the mouth is open. Some people say that is an invitation for evil spirits to enter. If the sneeze is really hard, someone can sneeze his or her soul across the room. With all these possibilities, a strong blessing of some sort is clearly called for. Have you ever *not* said "God bless you" after someone sneezes? Many people use the German word *gesundheit* (ga-zunt-hite) instead.

Just in case anyone thinks this is a recent superstition, a Roman writer reported that the emperor Tiberius "was punctilious in blessing the sneezes of others."

Superstitions at Work and Play

People in all walks of life act in accordance with superstitious beliefs. How many times have you thought "Step on a crack, break your mother's back" while walking, and avoided stepping on those "backbreaking" sidewalk cracks?

Superstitions invade every area of life. At home, some people do not count how many cookies they have just baked, so those they save will not go stale. Some people will not light three cigarettes from one match. For good luck, others always sweep dust balls into the middle of the room before they pick them up.

At work, some airline pilots carry lucky charms. Flight crews avoid saying the word *crash* before taking off. And most airline personnel believe that accidents come in groups of three. Some stock exchange members carry lucky pieces. London stock exchange members carry bent coins. But the coins must have been gifts and not received in change.

Sports Superstitions

Sports can be such "sudden death," win-or-lose situations that some people who make their living at sports tend to be superstitious.

Baseball players believe there are a certain number of hits in each bat. When the hits are used up, the bat is no good. Some coaches must kick the first-base plate bag before entering the box at the start of each game. Some players believe it is bad luck to sign autographs or have pictures taken before a game. Some never cross bats when laying two or more down. Seeing a cross-eyed woman before a game is bad luck, but seeing a load of empty barrels is good luck. Rubbing the bat with a piece of bone makes it stronger.

Boxers do not like to see a $10 bill or a hat on a couch or bed before a match. They do not like to be the first person in the ring, and they do not like to wear new shoes for an important match.

Golfers avoid "rubbing the luck off" a ball when the game is going well. Some throw bits of sand from the tee box onto the ground before teeing off. Tennis pro Martina Navratilova wears the same pair of diamond earrings during each tournament. She wears a turquoise tennis dress on the last day of a tournament. Gymnast Mary Lou Retton uses the same shampoo before every competition. Race-car drivers will not drive green cars, wear green, speak to anyone before a race who is wearing green, or even sign autographs with green pens.

Hockey players hit the shin pads of the goalies before their games. The Detroit Red Wings hockey team has a bizarre superstition. In 1952, a fan threw an octopus onto the ice as a good luck charm. The team won the eight games they needed to win the Stanley Cup. Ever since then, an octopus is put on the ice at the start of the season.

Actors' Superstitions

Possibly no other field of work is so full of superstitions as acting. A slip of the tongue or a change in timing can spell the difference between a hit and a flop.

Actors believe it is unlucky to whistle backstage, or say the last line of a play during a rehearsal. They consider the play *Macbeth* unlucky. They will not quotc lines from that play during the rehearsal of another play, or even mention the name of the play at any time. To most English actors, *Macbeth* is referred to as "the Scottish play." Actors do not wear the color yellow or the color black onstage, or allow a cross-eyed person backstage, or have peacock or peacock feather designs anywhere. Having someone else look into your mirror while you are putting on makeup is considered bad luck. But if an actor's shoes squeak during an opening scene, it is good luck.

Usually it is bad luck for a cat to cross the stage of a play in progress. But around the turn of the century, a cat walked across the Knickerbocker Theater's stage in New York City during a play called *Listen, Lester*. The play was a hit. The acting company adopted the cat, named it Lester, and sent it out for opening night of every play. If the cat took a stroll, the performance was sure to be a hit. Once the cat refused to go out, no matter how she was persuaded. Desperate, the leading lady carried Lester onstage in a bird cage! It was no use. The performance was a flop. "The cat could not be forced," the story goes. "Lester had to pick the hit herself."

Do You Know These?

Celtic countries have always had superstitions regarding the "little people." Some stories mention a lep-

rechaun or fairy with a pot of gold at the end of a rainbow. Less well known is a spirit called Will-o'-the-wisp. Will waits for night travelers and lures them off their paths by shining a small light just ahead. Eventually, the travelers drown in bogs or simply disappear forever.

Ancient Scots used to braid different-colored threads together to make either a charm or a curse. What each braid meant depended on the colors and what each stood for!

Native Americans thought a tiny demon lived in every kernel of popcorn. When the kernels were heated, the demons became enraged and popped out.

Long ago, at the end of a Jewish wedding, the bride and groom would try to step on one another's toes. Whoever succeeded first would be the dominant person in the family. Jewish families had a superstition that people died when they had used up the amount of words allotted then for their lifetime.

Every culture in every century has had its own superstitions. Many superstitions have lost their reasons for being carried out. Sometimes people do not even know how a superstition got started. Many superstitions end up being native customs or cultural traditions. It doesn't matter. As long as there are people, there will be superstitions of some sort, knock on wood!

For Further Reading

Aylesworth, Thomas G. *Animal Superstitions.* New York: McGraw-Hill, 1981.

Baldwin, Gordon Curtis. *Schemers, Dreamers, and Medicine Men.* New York: Four Winds Press, 1971.

Batchelor, Julie Forsyth. *Superstitious? Here's Why!* New York: Harcourt, Brace & World, 1954.

Boyd, Mildred. *Man, Myth, and Magic.* New York: Criterion Books, 1969.

Costikyan, Barbara. *Be Kind to Your Dog at Christmas.* New York: Pantheon Books, 1982.

Gregor, Arthur S. *Amulets, Talismans, and Fetishes.* New York: Scribner's, 1975.

Leach, Maria. *The Luck Book.* New York: Scribner's, 1964.

———. *The Soup Stone.* New York: Funk & Wagnalls, 1954.

Morrison, Lillian (comp). *Touch Blue.* New York: Crowell, 1958.

Sarnoff, Jane. *If You Were Really Superstitious.* New York: Scribner's, 1980.

———. *Take Warning!* New York: Scribner's, 1983.

Schwartz, Alvin (comp). *Cross Your Fingers, Spit in Your Hat.* Philadelphia: Lippincott, 1974.

Sullivan, George. *Sports Superstitions.* New York: Coward, McCann & Geoghegan, 1978.

Index